Vital Stream

Lucy Newlyn was born in Uganda and grew up in Leeds. She read English at Lady Margaret Hall, Oxford, where she also studied for her D. Phil, going on to become Lecturer then Tutorial Fellow at St Edmund Hall, Oxford. She taught English at St Edmund Hall for thirty-two years, published widely on English Romantic poetry, became a Professor in 2005 and retired in 2016. In addition to four books with Oxford University Press and (as editor) *The Cambridge Companion to Coleridge*, she has published two collections of poetry: *Ginnel* (Oxford Poets, Carcanet, 2005) and *Earth's Almanac* (Enitharmon, 2015). Newlyn's literary biography, *William and Dorothy Wordsworth 'All in Each Other'* (OUP, 2013) was chosen as a *TLS* Book of the Year. Her memoir *Diary of a Bipolar Explorer* was published in 2018 with Signal, and her book *The Craft of Poetry* (written entirely in verse) is forthcoming with Yale University Press. She now lives and writes in Cornwall.

Vital Stream

LUCY NEWLYN

CARCANET

First published in Great Britain in 2019 by
Carcanet Press Ltd
Alliance House, 30 Cross Street
Manchester M2 7AQ
www.carcanet.co.uk

Published in association with the Wordsworth Trust

A CfP catalogue record for this book is available from the British
Library

ISBN 978 1 78410 807 6

The publisher acknowledges financial assistance from Arts Council
England

Typeset in England by XL Publishing Services, Exmouth
Printed and bound in England by SRP Ltd, Exeter

For Sandie

'Is there not
An art, a music, and a stream of words
That shall be life, the acknowledged voice
Of life?'

(William Wordsworth, *Home at Grasmere*)

Contents

Preface

I have enjoyed *Vital Stream* immensely: initially reading about ten sonnets a day, and going back to Dorothy's *Grasmere Journal* as well as Lucy Newlyn's own *William and Dorothy Wordsworth: All in Each Other*. I think producing 135 convincingly modern sonnets, each fluent and alive, and with all their rich variations of form, is itself an astonishing technical achievement.

What's more, the sequence works brilliantly well as a biographical narrative of that momentous year 1802. Newlyn gives us not only a vivid celebration of those joyful 'spots of time', but also a subtle exploration of all those hidden anxieties, suppressed tensions and secret longings in that remarkable household. It is especially strong on the imagined rivalries (both domestic and literary) between Wordsworth and Coleridge; and on the eternally mysterious sibling love between William and Dorothy (as in the marvellous group of poems about the wedding ring). All provoking and intriguing speculations...

The unexpected appearances of Annette and Caroline Vallon, and of Charles Lamb and Sarah Coleridge, are wonderfully effective. Newlyn has given the story line its own natural ebb and flow, between plain daily events and intense visionary moments, which hold the reader in a steady rapt suspense. The lives and the landscapes flash up before us like vivid slides in a continuous poetic magic-lantern show.

I thought several individual sonnets were completely outstanding on their own. Among a dozen or so I would pick out 'William, seeking a perfect form'; 'Coleridge, on memories of 1798'; 'Dorothy, on Milton's influence'; 'Calais in August'; 'William, at Bartholomew Fair'; and 'Coleridge on the return of friends'. But there are many others.

Finally I read the whole sequence through in one go, and think that it would be greatly enhanced by being read out loud on radio. I do hope a producer can be found.

All in all, *Vital Stream* is a captivating act of dramatic and poetic re-invention.

Richard Holmes

Introduction

Vital Stream is a sequence of 135 sonnets which unfold in chronological order. It focuses on six extraordinary months in 1802, a threshold year for William and Dorothy Wordsworth. Parted when they were very young, the siblings had eventually set up home together in their native Lake District, where they were to remain for the rest of their lives. They had been settled in Grasmere for two years when William became engaged to a family friend, Mary Hutchinson. There followed an intense period of re-adjustment for all members of their circle. The Peace of Amiens was declared in March 1802: this enabled the Wordsworths to cross over the Channel to Calais in the summer. Here William would end his former liaison with Annette Vallon (which had been interrupted by the declaration of war ten years earlier) and meet for the first time his illegitimate daughter Caroline. His marriage to Mary in Yorkshire took place in October, immediately after which he returned home to Grasmere with his sister and his wife.

During the spring and summer of 1802, the Wordsworth siblings wrote some of their most beautiful poetry and prose; these were their last months of living alone, and much of their writing had an elegiac quality. In addition to anxieties in their own household, there were tensions with Coleridge, whose marriage was rapidly deteriorating at this time. Drawing on detailed knowledge of letters, poems, notebooks, and journals, *Vital Stream* explores thoughts and feelings about love, family bonds, friendship and creativity within the Wordsworth circle. The title of the sequence refers not just to the bodies of moving water which the siblings saw on their travels, but to the fluid quality of their relationships, conversations and creative processes.

Why sonnets? William Wordsworth discovered the power of Milton's sonnets during 1802, and this year saw him writing some of his greatest sonnets on political and personal themes. (He later developed the sonnet sequence as a medium for peripatetic writing in a collection celebrating the River Duddon.) Dorothy Wordsworth never wrote sonnets, though she did write a number of poems, and the Grasmere Journal has poetic qualities; indeed she described herself on one occasion as 'more than half a poet'. *Vital Stream* attends to the flow of creativity between brother and sister, finding the sonnet an appropriate medium for soliloquies and dramatic lyrics organised as narrative episodes. Using a variety of sonnet rhyme-schemes – Petrarchan, Spenserian, Shakespearian, *terza rima,* Meredithian, Harrisonian, and curtal – the sequence is both a tribute and a tributary to the Wordsworths' shared body of writings.

*

The sonnets in this sequence are best read aloud, and ideally they would be performed as a radio play. As dramatic monologues they offer parallel internal meditations (and sometimes conversations), alternating between ten characters. In their handling of iambic pentameter, they emphasise the expressiveness of spoken language, following a long sonnet-tradition that stretches back through Tony Harrison, Hopkins, Wordsworth, Milton, Donne and Wyatt.

The poems offer an interpretation of events and relationships, not a strict biographical record; poetic licence has sometimes been allowed. Most of them are narrated in the first person, with the voices alternating between the following characters: William, Dorothy and John Wordsworth; Samuel Taylor Coleridge and his wife Sara; Mary Hutchinson and her sister Sara; Annette Vallon and her daughter Caroline; Charles Lamb. The titles indicate who is speaking. (A small number of sonnets are narrated in the third person. Where this is the case, no name appears in the title to identify its speaker.)

Where a date appears in the title of a sonnet, this indicates that an entry in Dorothy Wordsworth's Grasmere Journal has prompted it; I have sometimes followed the phraseology of D.W.'s journal entries closely, but more often loosely. (She habitually used the abbreviation 'Wm' for William, and I have preserved this convention in several cases.)

There are six un-rhyming sonnets in the sequence which were composed as 'cut-ups' or 'centos', using phrases from notebooks and letters; I have identified cases of this method in the notes at the end of the book. Caroline Vallon (aged 9) also speaks in sonnet form but following none of the recognised sonnet rhyme-schemes. There are places where I have taken liberties with traditional sonnet forms to create particular effects.

Epigraphs have been used to anchor the sonnets in literary and biographical contexts. In order to keep academic references to a minimum, the sources for epigraphs are provided in the end-notes, where essential biographical information is also given. There are numerous other allusions within the sonnets; I have occasionally provided end-notes to identify the most essential of these.

PART ONE

A nest we build together

It was a threatening cold misty day
As we set off from Eusemere, the lake rough
And the wind furious, seizing our breath.
We saw a plough working, a boat at play
And a thick belt of daffodils stirring
Like a busy highway along the shore –
Then more and more of them, and yet more.
Some reeled and danced in the wind's whirring,
Some rested their heads for weariness.
Across the lake and within each stormy bay
The tossing waves sounded like the sea.
All was alive in the wind's restlessness
As we continued our homeward journey,
And throughout this day of celebration
There was universal animation.
I the one thing anxious, stunned, solitary.

Have I not reason for trepidation
On this stormy wind-thrashed ominous day,
Of all things the most vexed and lonely
'Mid Nature's general agitation?
My birthday passed (and with it half my life),
I am already 'husband', father, brother –
Soon to see my daughter and my lover,
For ever bonded to my future wife.
All is fixed: our wedding date decided.
Relieved of course by England's peace with France
I am in turmoil, with a troubled sense
Of loyalties unequally divided.
Firm and forthright, my sister strides ahead,
Her eyes turned from the dark and louring hills
To rest her gaze on the dancing daffodils,
The golden dancing daffodils, instead.

The becks among the rocks were all alive.
Wm showed me a mossy streamlet,
Remembering how when we first arrived
He liked its green track in the snow. We sat
For a while looking at the restful vale
Where crows flew in the sun white as silver,
Like thin shapes of water passing over
The smooth fields. By the time we climbed the wall
Rydal was in its own evening brightness,
We on the last leg of our journey home.
Bit by bit, shimmering at dusk under the moon,
Its small round isle a mound of darkness,
Grasmere came in view. We found our garden
Almost other-worldly in the twilight,
Our cottage waiting quietly for night,
Our own dear parlour hidden safe within.

If I could find, if I could only find
A tranquil spot in which to settle here
So I might think without my sister near
To sense the swaying of my restless mind…
I must be loyal and I would be kind
To all three women, but begin to fear
My work and way of life will cost them dear.
How selfish I have been, how blind.
The home I offer cannot be the home
My father would have wanted me to make.
We dwell in our aloneness and we roam
These hills and valleys for each other's sake,
Our spirits scattering like flecks of foam
Tossed to and fro on an unruly lake.

DOROTHY, ON DWELLING

'Then darkness came,
Composing darkness, with its quiet load
Of full contentment...'

All our homecomings bring back the day
We first arrived here, that bleak December
Two years ago in Grasmere. Remember
The house at nightfall in the gloom, the way
We walked uncertainly from room to room
In semi-darkness; how the chimney smoked,
How rough and rocky the back garden looked,
Our plans for a climbing pathway? Soon
This rented cottage came to seem like home.
We had prematurely parted and moved
So often, lived in houses we both loved,
But *this* place we could truly call our own.
Already now it has answered our longing
For the life together we freely chose –
Not a property (we have none of those)
But a dwelling-place, a way of belonging.

WILLIAM REMEMBERS

I pace the pathway searching for a rhyme
But find my brain distracted, overcast.
There is no spot, no present point in time
That is not saturated with the past.
I owe my fealty to boyhood years
And she to years in which I did not feature;
We are as sundered in our hopes and fears
As any living solitary creature.
And yet our home now teems with memories
Which serve to bond us to a place not ours –
How could they fail to reassure and please,
When they reflect so many happy hours?
Oh grant us peace, and may we never fail
To love the beauty of this tranquil vale.

We live alone but blessed with four or five
Dear friends, devoted to this peaceful spot –
Our love for Grasmere honoured, brought alive
In prose and verse. The little garden plot
Which John in our first year was keen to tend,
The grove of firs he paced as if on deck
And where, with thoughts of him, we bend
Our own steps as we view the distant lake,
The hut near Easedale Tarn, the waterfall
Which tumbles in the hidden dell, the fine lone
Rydal walk that Mary loves so well,
The path that ambles round the vale (yes, known
To Coleridge, but cherished long before
He came to dwell, our neighbour in this place),
All these attachments – and a thousand more –
We daily celebrate, and gladly trace.

Every spring, every stream and waterfall
Throughout this valley has sustained our love.
There is no silent tarn or roaring ghyll,
No stony shore, no mossy dripping cove
Left undiscovered. We are never still.
Like flowing water or like clouds we move,
Un-resting 'mid the solitary hills.
Together and apart we daily rove
From rugged moorland to small garden plot.
Like tiny springs, then threads of trickling water,
We start on high, and wander there bemused –
Growing more certain as we reach this spot
Then rushing strong as we approach each other
To merge at last and deeply interfuse.

The Spring is here. We are preparing
For Mary to arrive. What will this mean
For how we spend each day, our calm routine
Of walking, writing, reading, gardening?
She is our friend, we have relied on her for years –
I can think of nobody we could love
More dearly. What does my agitation prove
But the selfishness of a sister's fears?
Once wedded they will need a private room,
So when she comes I must politely move
Out of my own room to the floor above
And make her welcome in her married home.
Is it jealousy, an incurable
Need to cling to joys that we have known,
Which makes the thought of being there alone
So chilling and so unendurable?

WILLIAM, ON SHARING MEMORIES

'She gave me eyes, she gave me ears;
And humble cares, and delicate fears;
A heart, the fountain of sweet tears;
And love, and thought, and joy.'

Since March, with the awakening spring,
Dreams of my dear Annette have haunted me
And my deepest longings are for Mary –
But my sister's ministry is all I sing.
Eight years have been and gone since she and I
Were re-united, yet until today
I could never bring myself to say
It feels essential to have her nigh!
Our childhood garden has been on my mind:
Is it *heimweh*, heart-sickness, a pining
For our lost familial home, that brings
It back to me so clearly? Oh! To find
A method for recovering pleasures
That still lie hidden, buried deep within,
And catch them butterfly-like on a pin,
Lest we lose what our heart most treasures!

DOROTHY, ON DEAD TIMES

'A little prattler among men' he calls me!
But I was nurtured far from home, among
Both boys and girls– a large and rowdy throng.
He and I have managed separately
For many years...we have few memories
In common; so we routinely walk,
Observe, describe, and with our daily talk
Accumulate a lasting store of these.
We trust they will prepare us both for loss
Or further separation. Our means
Are meagre – and will be always. Wm leans
On me for stories. I gather them like moss,
Leaves, twigs and feathers for a nest
We build together, helping each other –
As any sister would (or brother)
For the one they have loved truest, longest, best.

The wound from parting when we were so small
Has never healed. In dreams her tiny frame
Is snatched from me, and I must take the blame.
Our mother dead, life at a sudden stall,
I hear her shocked voice call and call and call.
We shared our infancy, we shared our name,
But life would never be the same again:
Time intervened with its impervious wall.
Then after many years we tore it down
And I beheld her, wild and fair and free,
To womanhood now fully grown;
Well-read, content either to walk with me
Or ramble in the mountains on her own –
More precious than a friend could ever be.

DOROTHY IMAGINES THE FUTURE

And when the nest fills up, where will I go?
There is no better home; I have no other
Than this one I have made here with my brother.
But could I stay for ever, even so?
I fear the future. Most of all I fear
The loss of solitude – my time alone
Disturbed or spoiled; the seeds of anger sown
By sounds of love-making not far from here.
Our walls and floors are thin. I will be able
To hear the lovers move. Birds in their nest
Will have more privacy than they at best.
Hark how they chirp and baby-babble:
Must I, his fond companion now for years,
Try in some way to shut the noises out –
Turn a blind eye to what they are about,
Pretend that I feel nothing, block my ears?

WILLIAM'S PROMISE

'Where'er my footsteps turned,
Her voice was like a hidden bird that sang…'

Dear Dorothy, know that for evermore
I am your faithful brother, and will repay
The debt of gratitude I owe – each day,
Each year, will never knowingly foreswear
Or slight you, nor depreciate the care
That is your due. We would have you stay;
Together we will make one family.
Your life will not be wasted as you fear.
In the name of our dead parents and of all
That we hold dear from early infancy,
I solemnise this promise – and may you
Be with us always. I dedicate these small
Bequests to you, believing poetry
Will prove as I am: steadfast, loyal, true.

*'William lay, & I lay in the trench under the fence – he with
his eyes shut & listening to the waterfalls & the Birds. There
was no one waterfall above another – it was the sound of
waters in the air – the voice of the air. William heard me
breathing & rustling now & then but we both lay still, &
unseen by one another – he thought it would be as sweet thus to
lie in the grave, to hear the peaceful sounds of the earth & just
to know that ones dear friends were near.'*

Her brother lay, and she lay – separate,
Unseen by each other, as if interred,
Both hushed, both listening. She must wait
To know for certain whether he had heard
Her breathings, her rustlings, and to translate
His feelings lying near her into words:
'He thought', she wrote, 'it would be as sweet…'
How much was said aloud, how much inferred?
He'd stayed still as an infant in the wood,
Provoking her to think that he was dead:
'Entombed alive under the mossy sod
By robins' he might just as well have said
For all the solace that it brought her –
Remembering how then and there
Amid the noise of rushing water
Her sobs had mingled with the voice of air.

WILLIAM DREAMS ABOUT ANNETTE VALLON

'Heard the cuckow today this first of May'

In the night she came to me again
And though I pleaded with her not to stay
She stayed, and I could hear her clearly say
That she was here, and here she would remain
Till the first cuckoo's song in May
To lie with me where we had always lain
All day all night in that same bed of pain
Until the unborn child had gone away.
Her English words were plain, but in my dream
Our only child lay breathing, sleeping
Between us, so I knew we were in France.
Then there came a muffled sound, like a stream
Underground, or a woman far off weeping –
And I woke as the cuckoo called out, once.

All yesterday and then again today
We were peaceful, looking at the prospect,
So vision-like I was resigned to it.
The birds went about us on all sides: skobbys,
Robins, bullfinches, and crows now and then –
We knew they were there by the beating air.
We lingered till light of day was going,
Loughrigg Fell the most distant hazy hill;
Then came nearer copses, the round field's swell,
And slipping in between, the cool of Grasmere.
Oh, the beauty, greener than any green
Of the vale! Two ravens circled, way up high:
The sun shone upon their bellies and wings
Long after there was no light to be seen.
The sky was cloudless, three solitary
Stars in the blue vault, the landscape fading.

WILLIAM, ARS POETICA

> *'thy breath,*
> *Dear sister! was a kind of gentler spring*
> *That went before my steps...'*

The year advances. Now the days are mild
My sister has been out collecting mosses,
Uprooting violets and primroses
Where'er she finds them growing in the wild
And with the busy gladness of a child
Re-planting seedlings in bare crevices
Throughout our garden, whose rude surfaces
Will swarm with life once they have all been filled.
Just so, from her daily observations
(In living speech, sometimes in written prose)
I take small cuttings and make transplantations:
No words more fresh or natural than those
Used in spontaneous conversation –
From whose animating roots verse springs and grows.

DOROTHY, ON THE PRESENT

Every day now my brother is writing
About wild flowers and childhood, birds
In the garden, butterflies, the sounds of spring.
All my images are turned to words.
In recent verses he is thanking me
For what I give him, moments we have known,
As if composing us an elegy.
Must even present joys be set in stone?
There are sounds and impressions before time
Turns them to poetry; there are sensations
Too precious to be chiselled out in rhyme.
Living things in rapid fluctuation
Are remembered through the form we
Give them, whether written, thought or said.
I channel these as they are flowing through me,
Prizing each moment before it is dead.

I wonder is there somewhere to be found
A form of verse so like a drop of dew,
So delicately turned, so smooth and round
(Containing ev'ry circumambient hue
Within its shining bound) it can imbue
Our thought with water's clarity,
A glass for what we hold eternal, true;
Translucent, with the endless purity
Of mountain brooks, the flawless unity
Of a reflected world in miniature;
That even in its trembling brevity
Might gather to itself a quiet store
Of certitude and hang there poised, replete
With meaning – self-sustained, complete?

DOROTHY, ON COLLABORATION

My journal prompts him to write, sometimes
At once, but it means more than this to me:
With the day's rhythms, not the rule of rhymes,
I germinate the seeds of poetry.
At first, excited by my words, he follows
Them too closely – not quite breaking free
Of their immediacy; when allowed
To breathe, his verse grows naturally.
What is this force, this vital stream that flows
Between us, but our love and sympathy?
Poor dear Coleridge finds it comes and goes;
Yet still it is a power we feel, all three.
Whatever changes, whatever else we lose,
Our writing-current remains swift and strong.
In the undulations of verse and prose
We commingle and are borne along.

PART TWO

We are not solitary

At Greta Hall there is persistent strife.
Poor Coleridge flees daily, bringing news
Of misery with his resentful wife:
All joy is gone, he has none left to lose.
Unhinged by laudanum, desire and grief
He wanders aimlessly about. In lieu
Of death he feels a longing deep as life
To be truly loved – his natural due:
'Natural as the way that Coniston Fells
Climb upwards, step by step, into the blue,
Then drop away in silence through bare dales
To green secluded valleys…' As if on cue
The lake of Grasmere cradled in its vale
Comes suddenly, serenely, into view.
He digresses – his eye darts somewhere else;
He waves; he's off to look for something new.

COLERIDGE, WALKING ALONE

'Every man his own path-maker'

Half tipsy, all objects become interfused.
The river curves like an S rudely made
By a tremulous hand; the rocks seem to put on
A vital semblance. The thrush, gurgling, quavering,
Shoots forth long notes then short emissions
As if pushing up against a stream; the trout
Leaping in the sunshine spreads concentric
Circles of light on the bottom of the river.
Grysdale Tarn rolls towards its outlet
Like the sea, the gust on the broad beck
Snatching up the water. Every time
The gust comes, the sun setting on the hill
Behind me makes a rainbow in the spray
Which falls upon me, *lownded* in the rock, like rain.

By the roadside, on the way to Grasmere
From the northerly town of Keswick,
Lies Wythburn – a still, solitary lake
Whose smooth surface is broken only where
Herons dive, or water-insects skate. Slow
Clouds move across a brightly mirrored sky
Or imperceptibly shiver and sway
In the huge darkness of Helvellyn's shadow.
Set back from the shore at a point midway
Between two poets' neighbouring homes
Is a trysting-place, the tall 'Rock of Names',
Where we and our loved ones often stray.
We have carved our initials here with a knife
And sometimes when we meet to read or talk
We chip away to make a clearer mark:
Close friends who claim in rock immortal life.

UNDER HELVELLYN, 4 MAY

*'We looked at the Letters which C carved in the morning. I
kissed them all. Wm deepened the T with C's penknife.'*

They rest by the wayside several times,
Their breath coming in a little shorter.
Coleridge waves, crossing the beck to them
From the Wythburn side of the water.
Now they walk in varied formations –
Sometimes a pair, the third lagging behind,
Sometimes all three together, their motion
Slower. Beneath that purple crag, a wild
Solitude. A bird flying round and round
Transparently – thin as a moth. No shade
On this sweltering day until they find
A moss-cushioned rock rising from the bed
Of the river. There they lie, repeating
Verses, eating dinner; at the Rock they part
With C, wish him well till their next meeting.
Then sit on a wall, nursing his broken heart.

'He is our friend, yet he seems not to know
How much we care for him.' She bowed her head
To think of what his sorrow made her dread.
Her brother sighed and nodded. 'It seems so.
His will has snapped; he seems a broken man.
He has no spine; he veers and veers about
Much like a flimsy weathercock in doubt,
And says he can no more – though he still can.'
'What should we do, what does he need?' she asked –
'There is no end to what my heart would give
If we could help him live as he should live.
We can still try, however we are tasked.'
'Too late – already far too late' he said.
'I fear for him. The worst is yet to come.
We give him loaves and he picks up a crumb;
We offer hope, it might as well be dead.'

To love is to know, or at least to imagine
That you know. What is strange to you
Cannot be loved. My Sara is all strange,
And the *Terra Incognita* always
Lies under the frozen poles. I am heart-starved
By her selfishness. She is cold and calm
And deep as frost: morally frigid,
Paralysed in all tangible ideas
And sensations. Oh! The love-killing effect
Of ill-tempered speeches, recriminations.
I was once a volume of gold leaf, rising
And riding on every breath of Fancy.
Now, beaten back into weight and density,
I remain squat and square on the earth.

How suddenly, within a single year,
The course of married life is warped and changed:
His constitution marred beyond repair
By laudanum, his darkened mind deranged.
Am I to blame for want of sympathy?
Is it *my* fault that we find ourselves in debt
When he spends his days either in apathy
Or chasing all the pleasure he can get?
If for a little while he could be tranquil
And complete his tasks instead of talking,
If he could sit in his study, calm and still,
Instead of all this walking, walking, walking,
We could untangle this atrocious mess.
If only he would spend less time at Grasmere
And pay attention to his children here,
We might regain our fragile happiness.

'Every generous mind feels its Halfness and cannot think
without a Symbol – neither can it love without something that
is at once to be its symbol, & its other Half'

Asra, most innocent and full of love,
Compassionate comforter, loved as no
Woman has been beloved! The secret sign
You gave was the abrupt creation
Of a moment – discovered as by a flash
Of lightning, the strike of a horse's shoe
Or a flint, in utter darkness. One *look*
Of the eyes, seen only by the person
On whom it worked, and by him only
To be seen. Since then you have been my life,
My soul, my being. Every single thought,
Image, perception, was no sooner *itself*
Than it became *you*, or a symbol of you.
I have played with them as with your shadow.

SARA HUTCHINSON, ON BEING LOVED BY
COLERIDGE

To be the object of his devotion
Flattered me at first. But no, I never
Sought nor wanted this intense emotion,
Which like a gushing mountain river
Overflows all bounds. Once, to receive
His verse and letters was to be his Muse;
And if his statements were to be believed
He wanted nothing further than to choose
A trusted friend as comforter of all
His woes. But now he bitterly confides
That marriage is a dark and deadly pall.
No-one need tell me that there are more sides
To this story. I feel for him of course
But his obsession has become a blight.
Overwhelmed by the increasing force
Of his attentions, I deplore my plight.

*'The unspeakable comfort to a good man's mind – nay, even
to a criminal – to be understood – to have some one that
understands one – & who does not feel that on earth no one
does. The Hope of this – always more or less disappointed, gives
the* passion *to Friendship.'*

Unhappy me, with no one to bewail
My woes, or understand my inmost
Needs and longings. Yes, my Muse and wife
Have much in common; thereby hangs a tale
Of ironic fusion. Its disastrous cost
Will be no less than *wreckage* of my life.
If I whisper 'Sara' softly in my sleep,
Which of these star-crossed women is the most
Betrayed? My hopeless passion is the *thief*
Of time, contentment, rest: a yawning deep
      Below a treacherous reef.

WILLIAM, REASSURING COLERIDGE

'When thou dost to that summer turn thy thoughts,
And hast before thee all which then we were...'

Yes, we will remain your friends forever.
How can you doubt it? Think back, once again,
To Nether Stowey and Alfoxden –
That year we had, all three of us together.
Nothing can destroy our love, or sever
The bonds that formed between us then.
But how can we help or comfort you, when
You see our steady life as a tether?
Remember how you greeted us that day –
Bounding high over the gate at Racedown,
Your first encounter with dear Dorothy.
How quickly then the seeds of love were sown,
How soon they grew into a fertile tree.
Why must you forsake us and go off alone?

'never elsewhere in one place I knew
So many nightingales…'

I well remember those walks near Stowey,
The nightingales sweet-singing in the woods,
The glow-worms lighting up for Dorothy,
The full moon gazing at us while we stood
All three together, silent on the bridge –
My baby sleeping, peaceful in his cot,
The houses hushed at night, the quiet village.
It was a magical, enchanted spot!
But all is vanished now, entirely lost –
Our paradise in Somerset exchanged
For this pale imitation of the past,
My marriage wrecked, me from myself estranged.
I wake each dawn to overwhelming beauty;
Almighty Skiddaw towers there the same –
With me below still, chafing at my duty,
And only unrequited love to blame.

WILLIAM ATTEMPTS TO CONSOLE

'As high as we have mounted in delight
In our dejection do we sink as low.'
The nightingale sings gladly even though
We may not always hear her music right
Or see her gleaming eyes at dead of night.
As streams are sometimes hindered in their flow
So do the mind's moods falter and move slow.
Why denigrate what passes out of sight?
You are endowed with a creative gift:
In verse you re-possess the things you lose,
Not least if they like fragile flotsam drift
Or seem too humble for your lofty Muse.
Treasure what passes; soon your mood will lift
And you will make the happiness you choose.

He slammed the door; he stamped off in the wind.
What can be salvaged from our morning walk
Now that my brother paces in the dark,
Morose and anxious, fretting for his friend?
Clear images are swarming, quickening:
One cold wet day last year with dearest Mary
I watched the sudden sunshine in a tree
And tried out various ways of likening
Two forms of evanescence to each other –
'Spirit of water…sunshiny shower…'
If only I could tap their healing power
And give it like a tonic to my brother…
Words, only words, would do him any good.
I'd set them out like stepping-stones in prose
(No other miracles for now but those).
I would include some verses if I could.

COLERIDGE LETS OFF STEAM

*'better to do nothing
than nothings'*

Excited, manly, driven, gifted, keen,
He scribbles daily. She only has to mention
What she has seen to him in conversation –
A passing beggar, say, a *pretty* scene –
And off he goes, transforming it to verse
Without a moment's hesitation,
As if the precepts of association
Were all that mattered in the universe!
Was it for this we *traipsed* the lovely hills
Of Somerset, plotting a revolution
For humankind? Does the real solution
To war and oppression, all of Europe's ills,
Lie in the *flimsy* wings of butterflies,
The *nuptial* light of glow-worms, the *tiny*
Stars of celandines? Ye Gods, what a *puny*
Mite the mind is when brought down to size!

'There is a sympathy in streams: "One calleth to another"'

There is no solitude more desolate
Than the chasm left by friendship's waning:
The first signs of involuntary hate
Are quickly camouflaged by social feigning,
Only to deepen and intensify.
What would it be to live here side by side
Without his love, beholding the same sky
From separate spots, and nowhere to abide
But our own occluded sanctuary?
What would the hills, the moon, the woods and lakes
Mean, if one were truly solitary?
There is a sympathy in living becks
Which call across the moors to one another.
Let us do likewise still, brother to brother.

What is it that these women think they see
In Wordsworth, once my dear and trusted friend,
Who turns his back to leave me frightened, lonely,
And brings all joy to an untimely end?
Are there some passions that he cannot quell?
Is one devoted handmaid not enough,
That he must have a doting wife as well?
And what about his former bit of fluff?
Imagine Town End as a meek hareem –
Three wives is surely ample; must suffice
To constitute a selfless loving team
And service all the poet's needs. How nice:
He presses hidden stops of amorous art.
All women blend in his capacious heart.

'These little Angel children (woe is me!)
There have been hours when feeling how they bind
And pluck out the wing-feathers of my mind,
Turning my Error to Necessity,
I have half-wished they never had been born.'

Dorothy is making frocks for Derwent,
Nearly two years old; and the verse for Hartley
Is complete: a token for their absent
Friend, who has been dejected lately.
What's she thinking, sat in the parlour
Threading her needle, sewing the sleeve?
Does her mind run on her childless future,
Keeping home at Town End? Or does she grieve
For poor Coleridge's children, who pluck out
The wing-feathers of his mind? 'Dearest friend,
How can you begin to question or to doubt
My feelings? A father's love can never end –
It is the one and only unchanging thing…'
He'd stood there in the doorway as he said it.
She remembered his infant Berkeley dying
And fell silent. No one could mend it.

SARA COLERIDGE SPECULATES ABOUT HER HUSBAND

If I could trace the origin and cause
Of our affliction, whose fault would it be?
When Berkeley died, he was in Germany.
He might have shared the grief that daily claws
At both our hearts today if straight away
He had come home. He was immovable,
As if already then insensible:
Why not return? What was it made him stay?
If he had shown his feelings, might we still
Have known some small domestic happiness,
Or would it always have been just like this?
He blames his misery on 'Christabel'
And claims if it had never been rejected
He would be writing verses daily now –
Instead of which the seeds of envy grow.
Each time he sees his 'friend' he is dejected.

A starling self-incaged and always
In the moult, my whole note is 'tomorrow'.
My thinking has unhealthy vividness,
Like reverie. I could not be happy
Without Hartley, whose rule from infancy
Might have been 'Not me alone! My thoughts
Are my darlings!' Friends are burthensome
To him, excepting me: I can sympathise
With his wild fancies and suggest others
Of my own. He wonders 'what if there were
Nothing? – A whole world of darkness, coldness,
And yet nothing dark or cold?' How quickly
Like patchy clouds skimming across Skiddaw
Questions *scud* and metaphors are blown!

DOROTHY, SKY-GAZING, 6 MAY

'I see the old Moon in her lap, foretelling
The coming-on of rain and squally blast.
And oh! that even now the gust were swelling,
And the slant night-shower driving loud and fast!'

We walked to and fro in the twilight until
Darkness fell. I imagine Coleridge
Was watching tonight's capsized moon as well –
His elbows resting on the window ledge,
Leaning out to sniff the mountain air…
She had the old moon in her arms again
But not so clearly as the night before.
(When I think of good Sir Patrick Spens
And his fellow sailors drowned at sea
I wish our brother John were with us here.)
We are not solitary, we have three
Shadowy partners who are sometimes near.
We have watched many moons together
From positions all round Grasmere,
Jointly foretelling rain or stormy weather.
But never so nervously, with so much to fear.

'W.W. M.H. D.W. S.H.'

Where has it gone, the feeling that was
Four loves mingled into one, a stream
Moving softly, whose perpetual flow
Was *Life*, not Change, so translucent
As not to be seen, its source always hidden
And murmuring of a shadowy world?
I am like a mother listening for the sound
Of a still-born child – or a blind Arab
Straining to hear steps in the wilderness.
Yet now a waterfall dances where a leaf
Is still attracted, still repelled, below.
My love for Asra is a spring, its tiny
Cone of loose sand ever rising and sinking
At the bottom, but without a wrinkle.

PART THREE

An altercation

It snows today, as it did at Christmas.
The men at Town End and at Greta Hall
Are gloomy, taking turns to be unwell,
Holed-up indoors, sending each other letters.
After a sleepless night, William lies in.
I sit mending stockings, watch the snow,
Read Shakespeare, bake some bread, resolve to go
To Keswick after sad words this evening.
Two days later and still unwell, William
Walks with me as far as Wythburn water.
A lark and thrush are singing by the Greta.
Our friend is ailing, dazed by laudanum.
After two days he returns with me
To Grasmere. I am exhausted now
And take myself to bed fearing a row
While upstairs the men converse excitedly.

Away with these divisions between
Philosophy and lyric verse: our true
Object is wonder. Of all men how can you
(Who know that the One Life is felt and seen
In *all* things, from bare crags to valleys green)
Despise the wonders that are full in view
Around you, each day rewarding new
Discoveries with pleasures deep and keen?
The botanist, the chemist and the poet
Have this much in common: rapt attention
To detail, obsession in the pursuit
Of knowledge, reverence for creation.
Why disparage the means whereby your art,
Like science, can prompt revelation?

COLERIDGE RESPONDS

I look around me here and feel no joy,
No animation: true ebullience springs
From deep within. The living world can bring
No consolation. Nature is a toy,
A tawdry gewgaw fashioned for a boy
To play with, as a nightingale might sing,
Neglectful of our human suffering:
Gold adulterated with base alloy.
Everything we see, hear, touch and feel
Is traduced by our intrusive 'I',
Which makes this haven a very hell
To one whose lot like mine is misery.
Ask your leech-gatherer on his lonely fell:
Try telling *him* to 'wonder' at the sky.

WILLIAM EXPLAINS

'My' leech-gatherer looks mostly downward
Stirring his muddy pond, but he is not
Dejected; he accepts his grinding lot
And searches endlessly, still moving onwards,
Receiving a pittance for his mean reward.
Hard work consumes him. He may care not a jot
For beauty. He may not give a damn what
You and I will make of his firm, stoic words –
And we can no more help his poverty
Than we can thwart that knave Napoleon
In his march towards blind sovereignty;
But we can each bear witness to this man's
Resolution, and from his dignity
There is much that we can also learn.

Have you learnt nothing from your readers
About what is suitable to verse?
What do *they* care if the leech supply is scarce
Or vagrants strike you as moral leaders?
You will bore us if you do not heed us.
Why use stanza after stanza to rehearse
Minutiae when you could keep it terse?
You counsel us; but you must surely need us?
Mark my words, poetry differs in kind
And degree from prose. Some keep a journal,
But the language of verse is more refined.
If you descend into the diurnal
You sacrifice true vision, reach of mind.
Your themes are merely personal, *internal.*

I draw freely on my sister's journal
Because it sets down plainly and clearly
What touches all of us most nearly
And because it is a living chronicle
Of Grasmere Vale. It concerns real people
And records the incidents that really
Occur around us – weekly, monthly, yearly.
It is the very stuff of life and eternal.
Have you forgotten what I tried to do
In ballads? Is my plainness risible?
Must we deal only with what is long ago
And far away – sublime, invisible?
Regard Helm Crag. In verses, even so:
The most naked simplicity possible.

Dear friend, you forget that it takes *three*
To make a worthy collaboration.
Not so long ago our conversation
Led to a volume which included me.
Why is it so hard, now, for you to see
That the *other-worldly* makes a contribution
To your never-ending celebration
Of life and love, wholesome toil and family?
Like your stock-dove brooding over its own
Sweet voice, you have lately come to believe
That your household is self-sustaining.
I will not play pigeon, coo-cooing all alone,
Nor can delays with *The Recluse* deceive.
Like the nightingale I will go on plaining.

Still harping on that minor exclusion?
How long did you assume that we could wait
For your unfinished ballad? You were late,
And we were much bemused by your confusion.
You speak as if we suffered no intrusion;
As if you were still thriving, clear of debt,
As if your urgent deadlines could be met;
But this, despondent friend, is sheer illusion.
Already by two years ago you drifted –
Your work is something that you now bewail.
How can this long-established mood be lifted?
Your body and demeanour show you ail.
Because you are our friend, and greatly gifted,
We cannot bear to watch you while you fail.

COLERIDGE ACCUSES

I too am sad to sense the dissolution
Of all the aims in which I once invested.
I *had* hoped, though I was so tried and tested,
To find some tonic, remedy, solution.
That hope is gone. I see no resolution.
I have been bettered by you – bested.
My work is like a wave that breaks, *un-crested*.
Content to brush aside my contribution,
You point the finger *my* way; fail to see
That you betrayed our friendship and my trust.
There is no purpose we can now agree:
Our friendship is but *verdigris* and rust.
The bitterness I feel is part of me;
I will give voice to it because I must.

What would you have me say, and be, and do?
You burrow down, ever more deep inside
A den where no-one else would want to hide –
A cave that shields the shivering quick of you.
Come out into the lovely shimmering blue
Which canopies the mountains far and wide
And prowl about, divested of your pride,
Your lion's roar shrunk to a docile mew.
Gentled by beauty, you will feel the touch
Of happiness, like waves on sun-warmed sand.
You only need to look, and you will know
You are not everything, you are not much
Compared to what lies round you, close at hand –
An ever-changing everlasting flow.

COLERIDGE CONCLUDES

You see a world not open to my view,
A world that Hymen brightens with her veil.
You hear the singing of the nightingale,
A concert she composes just for you.
You feel with senses fresh and ever-new
You taste with palate that can never fail
You have no pain, your body cannot ail
You know more joy than I could ever do.
Remember though that marriage is a test.
Joy at this pitch can never be sustained:
Men choose the women they love dearest, best,
Only to find their way of life constrained.
Cocooned inside your cosy little nest
Be wary lest your mind is trapped and chained.

PART FOUR

Bidding goodbye

DOROTHY, IN THE ORCHARD, 28 MAY

All morning William has been walking
Backward, forward, hammering at a poem
That haunts him – muttering, as if talking
To someone who teases, tasks, or taunts him.
In the orchard, poised and balancing
On spindly branches that tremble, twist and bend,
The bullfinches are tumbling, dancing,
As if their acrobatic show will never end.
All around them under the apple trees
Lie blossoms from the twigs that they have shaken,
Newly fallen with a scattering of leaves.
A thick clump of gowans I have taken
From the lakeside is drooping now and fading;
Wild columbines are coming into beauty,
Vetches abundant, blossoming and seeding.
The air is mild, at evening it rains sweetly.

Can it be truly said and fully meant
That I am turning gradually stale,
That I decline, that all my days are spent
In feeble efforts and to no avail?
I seek some recompense, some rich reward.
My erstwhile friend's critique bears in on me
And wears my genial spirits down. Hard
Though I labour to perfect my verse, he
Finds it lacking in imagination –
And so I try once more to turn my mind
To *The Recluse,* my poem for the nation.
Oh, to indulge sheer beauty and to find
In all that is around us the repose
Which our unquiet spirits sought – and chose.

DOROTHY, ON MILTON'S INFLUENCE

Never have I seen my brother so excited
As he was by Milton's sonnets, read aloud
A week ago by me. At once ignited
He wrote a few himself. How manly, proud
And dignified he grew, no longer bowed
By doubt but borne aloft as if on strains
Of austere music. There and then he vowed
Devotion to a form that never wanes,
Renewing hope for Man's release from chains
And thus an end to one man's tyranny.
All the same, walking the quiet hills and lanes
With me, his verse still stirs with many
A soft melody; and in the hutch of night
Unnumbered glow-worms spill their faery light.

I feel compelled by a new form of verse,
One that will combine the rhythmic pleasure
Of a vigorous uplifting measure
With heroic language, muscular and terse.
Oh that my words might nourish, heal and nurse
All who, forfeiting their heart's best treasure,
Spend their days in wanton wasted leisure,
Despair, procrastination and remorse.
Coleridge my dearest friend I hear you.
Our aims are not forgotten: please believe
That everything which is your promised due,
All that we try jointly to achieve,
All that we deem purposeful and true,
Will triumph here and work a swift reprieve.

The glow-worms hide, the nightingales are dumb.
All fellow-creatures at this hour withdraw
Into the cavernous darkness of the moor
And only I still speak, though I am numb.
These fragments that I scribble are the notes
Sent from my inner self to those whose ear
I cannot hope to reach. They will not hear.
I am alone, building my soul in quotes
From intellects who have eternal life.
Their words are empty vessels until spoken
By one whom their past quandary has woken –
One who has felt their joy, their gloom, their strife.
Friend like no other, let my notebook be
A channel that will set their spirits free.

DOROTHY — A VETERAN CALLS AT TOWN END, 1 JUNE

Today an old man called, a grey-headed
Man who said he was a soldier.
His wife and children died in Jamaica.
On his shoulder he had a beggar's wallet
And a drab coat made of shreds and patches.
He was tall, and though his back was bent
He looked like someone used to being upright.
We talked a while; his words emerged in snatches.
'You are a fine woman' he said to me
When I gave him bacon and a penny.
After tea I went with Wm to Butterlip How.
The young oak leaves are all dry as powder.
When we came in we sat by the window
Alone, he with his hand on my shoulder,
Deep in love and silence: a blessèd hour.
We drew to the fire, ate broth for supper.

WILLIAM, ON READING ALOUD

'This is the spot: how mildly does the Sun
Shine in between the fading leaves!'

Sometimes she reads aloud, lulling me when
I am fractious as a child. In the spring
It was 'This is the spot' all over again –
Smoothly and steadily like the soothing
Lullaby a mother sings. Those are words
Of mine; she knows them now by heart,
Speaking them soft and low, as a bird
Croons sweetly tuneful to its single mate.
Later Shakespeare's pastoral plays
Have calmed us as the ending comes in sight
To our long unfettered summer days.
Shall we be willing to forego this rite
When I return with Mary, newly wed?
Who will watch me when I blow the candles out?
Will my sister fret, alone inside her bed,
A helpless orphan terrified by night?

'William observed that the full moon above a dark fir grove is a
fine image for the descent of a superior being'

The first halloo was like a human shout.
I felt surprised when it made a second call
(So tremulous and thin, so lengthened out)
To find it coming from a nearby owl.
The moon, moored low over the fir-grove
And not quite full, was among a company
Of steady island clouds, and the sky
All round was bluer than it was above –
A deeper much intenser shade of blue.
So did the moon 'descend', a higher being?
I saw it as a companion staying.
One night, hanging low over Silver How
It was like a thin gold ring snapped in two,
Shaven at the ends it was so narrow.
But clasped within and distinctly to be seen
Lay the full round body of a shadow-moon.

WILLIAM, ON REVISING 'THE LEECH-GATHERER',
14 JUNE

*'You speak of his speech as tedious: everything is tedious when
one does not read with the feelings of the author.'*

My drift is lost, even among my friends.
What hope, then, has it in the outside world
But through revision? I must make amends
For insights left un-glimpsed and truths untold.
A critic snipes at me from Gallow Hill,
No doubt egged on by Coleridge. Pulled
This way, that way, my loyalty is still
With ballads – but this plain unvarnished tale
(Which once I foolishly believed would fill
My readers' hearts with ruth) has clearly failed.
I bring, now, something different to my theme
And trust a shining message to unfold.
Oh for a touch of the visionary gleam
That glows from all things that we see in dream!

DOROTHY, ON WILLIAM'S CHANGE OF MIND

'When you feel any poem of his to be tedious, ask yourself in what spirit it was written.'

On finishing the first draft he began
To rally and was filled with glad relief
That it was done – but he was dashed when
Sara's letter like an unexpected thief
Stole all his confidence and self-belief.
His chronicle in verse has since dissolved
And though I try to fortify his faith
He seems un-settled still and un-resolved,
Taking his lead from readers less involved.
How quickly, like a beck swelled up by rain,
He speeds ahead now that my prose is shelved.
As if his verses, running clear and free again
After long drought, had need of this one shower
To change their course for ever, in the hour.

WILLIAM DIGESTS SOME GOOD NEWS, 20 JUNE

*'We walked upon our own path for a long time. We talked
sweetly together about the disposal of our riches... Mr and
Miss Simpson called. We told them of our expected good fortune.
We were astonished & somewhat hurt to see how coldly Mr
Simpson received it.'*

Two days have passed since the good news reached us:
Soon Lowther is to clear his cousin's debts!
Delivered now from dire financial threats
We talk of 'the disposal of our riches'.
How quickly the response of neighbours switches
From sympathy to envy – local bets
Against us are all lost; the family gets
From experience what wisdom teaches.
We will come soon into our inheritance,
The fortune that has been so long retarded,
But is the cost of our independence
That friends will be mistrustful, guarded?
Hard and bitter has been our endurance –
How unjust if we are thus rewarded.

On the Rock of Names my own initials come
Just after William's, to signify
His love for me and quietly confirm
A change in the settled order. Then why,
When letters pass between us, can we
Have no privacy? For several years
Now he has lived alone with Dorothy;
It would be natural to have some fears
As the wedding-day draws nigh. Do they feel
That for all my sympathy I will be
Intrusive, or that something strong and real
Will be stolen from us all, invisibly?
Or even that their happiness might cease
To thrive, once married relations start?
Oh, that there were more certainties to ease
A troubled and unsettled heart!

DOROTHY WATCHES THE SWALLOWS, 25 JUNE

Again they come, bustling and fluttering
Under my bedroom window – and meanwhile
He injures himself with altering
His poem for Mary. I am ill
In stomach from agitation. For her sake
He tosses and turns at night with worry:
This is his wedding-gift, he must make
It perfect – he says there is no hurry.
Two weeks ago, thinking it was done,
I made a copy in my neatest hand
But there were verses yet to come,
No sooner written than like cones of sand
They crumbled. And now a storm in the night
Has torn the swallows' nest from the wall
So that at day-break they are up and about,
Making do and mending, as must we all.

During the long summer days we have been
Preparing for Mary. Now the garden
Is clean and lush from the refreshing rain.
Butterflies settle among the laden
Laurel bushes, bright scarlet against green;
Birds dwell in the orchard, no fruit forbidden.
This is a blessèd spot, a tranquil scene:
Once our promised land, 'tis now our Eden.
But soon we must leave this precious slip
Of fertile ground. By the time that we return
The biting winds will have begun to strip
The bronze and yellow trees in autumn.
With every passing day as our French trip
Draws closer I desire to stay – yes, yearn
To stay for ever – safely in the grip
Of this small domestic patch of mountain.

DOROTHY'S FAREWELL, 7 JULY

'For two months now in vain we shall be sought:
We leave you here in solitude to dwell
With these our latest gifts of tender thought…'

The swallows have re-built their broken nest.
We went last night to the top of the hill
To see Rydale. The sky was dark and dull,
The vale solemn – all things quiet and at rest,
Helm Crag distinct. We ambled to and fro
On the White Moss path. There was a sky-like
Brightness on the lake: it was the Wyke
Cottage light at the foot of Silver How.
Some glow-worms were shining, bright though few.
O beautiful place! – Dear Mary, William –
It is Friday morning now, the horse is come,
I must give over and prepare to go,
Bidding goodbye to the swallows, the well,
The garden, roses, all. (They sang after
I was in bed, seeming to sing to each other,
Then settled as night fell.) I must go. Farewell.

WILLIAM, AFTER PARTING FROM COLERIDGE, 12 JULY

Tired though he is by his domestic trials
He was keen to see us safely on our way,
And walked with us for six or seven miles.
How could he know, or we ourselves foresee
How sad, how strained this last farewell would be?
We rested together by the roadside,
Each sunk in our own silent melancholy
Then brusquely parted.
                              Sudden, deep and wide
The gap between us as we watched him stride
Away, neither looking back nor waving,
A man possessed, a man who cannot bide.
As if our love had never been worth having,
As if a stream stopped flowing then and there,
Dammed beneath Blencathra's stony stare.

A QUESTION, 14 JULY

'We had a cheerful ride though cold, until we got to Stanemoor,
& then a heavy shower came on, but we buttoned ourselves up,
both together in the Guard's coat & we liked the hills & the
Rain the better for bringing us so close to one another – I never
rode more snugly.'

Coleridge is trying out analogies:
When two lives join, as in the confluence
Of rivers, are there *backward eddies*,
A kind of *churning* under the surface,
Or does one mighty current's influence
Have immediate sway? – In marrying,
Can selves *commingle* in a streamy essence?
Not far away, a coach is carrying
His friends from Stanemoor, where it's raining.
They're huddled together, snug and warm
Beneath the guard's overcoat, enjoying
The ride, the wind in their faces, freedom.
What would he think if he could see them now,
'All in each other', merged in life's swift flow?

At last we have arrived safe at the farm
Where we can rest, enjoy good food with friends.
The relaxation is a soothing balm
After long travel, and Sara's kindness mends
Our scattered spirits as the first day ends.
Nothing at all has changed, except dear
Mary, missing Coleridge; she sends
Her love. We do so wish that he was near –
But how would he behave if he were here?
What if he saw his Asra now and failed
To keep his love contained? How we all fear
For him, his work, his children, when he ails.
Most men are not themselves when deep in love.
Restraint must cure what time will not remove.

MARY, ON IMPENDING SEPARATION

Here they both are. For five days I enjoy
A brief foretaste of happiness, but soon
Our daily round of outings starts to cloy.
Tom notes the damaged crops; the rain streams down.
We stay inside, aware that time slips by
And still so much is pending, unresolved.
Will he be gone for long? Hard as I try
I feel excluded, want to be involved,
And cannot stop my foolish self from fearing
That he will once again be netted, chained.
The clock ticks. Now the final day is nearing
No plans are secret. All has been explained.
Oh, why must this French woman intervene
To spoil a union we have long foreseen?

This is our home from home, the place where all
Plans reach their long-delayed conclusion.
We had a short time here, a happy lull –
And now at last, to banish all confusion,
We go abroad. Dear Mary's durance
In the weeks to come will surely be
Extreme. Thus far she has shown patience
Well beyond the powers of ordinary
Women; she should not be asked for more.
While waiting loyally for our return,
Like many victims of this futile war
She will watch out for letters, pine, and yearn.
Fate takes me from her, as I was removed
Before from one who dearly, truly loved.

WILLIAM, DOROTHY, MARY

They watch the big hand on the clock creep round
And wonder what the coming weeks will bring.
Theirs is an ancient game of 'lost and found' –
A strange unspoken complicated thing.
They understand the rules of give-and-take
Established long before the stakes were seen,
And still adhered to for tradition's sake
Which none of them would dare to contravene.
The final stamp and seal must now be set,
The past be put to rest and new life started.
What risks they face and what rewards they get
Will not be known till after they are parted.
Hymen stands by, cards hidden from their eyes.
The fates, discreet, preserve a blank disguise.

PART FIVE

A turbulent month

DOROTHY, AFTER A SHORT STAY IN LONDON

*'the sun shone so brightly with such a pure light that there was
even something like the purity of one of nature's own grand
Spectacles.'*

How harshly after two months of preparing
The noise has broken over us! How slowly
We understand the sudden change – staring
From coaches, dazed and stunned by majesty,
Gliding ghostly thin around the city,
Silent 'mid the busy crowds of men.
For days my brother fretted anxiously,
Made speechless by the shocking raucous din:
Aware of me once and once only, when
We paused for a while on Westminster Bridge
To gaze upon the early morning scene
And I cried out for joy as at the edge
Of a small shining tarn in Westmorland –
Surprised by beauty, reaching for his hand.

Passive, I am swept along by the years'
Swift-flowing current, which lifts and carries
Me to the chalky cliffs of Dover. Tears
Steal one by one out of hiding, plain to see
In the glaring sunshine now that we are free
Of uproar, surrounded by rolling green.
Nine long summers have come between me
And the faithful husband I might have been,
Had not War like a jealous rival intervened.
O my love, my daughter, now a decade old,
What isolated times you must have seen,
Immured in France, a lone forsaken child.
Again your new-born face comes back to me –
Unknown, imagined, still about to be.

CALAIS IN AUGUST

'The town of Calais seemed deserted of the light of heaven, but there was always light, & Life, & joy upon the Sea.'

What did they find to fill their time each day,
Confined with Annette and her nine-year-old
Through four long weeks in sweltering Calais?
What vows were made, what narratives were told –
All four together strolling on the beach,
Their normal lives in Grasmere put on hold,
His wedding plans postponed and out of reach,
Observing day after hot day unfold;
Expecting lawyers' letters from Orleans,
In exile from Town End, the hills, the streams, the lake?
Did they regret the trip and dwell on dreams
Of happy marriage, lying wide awake
In their hot rooms, awaiting dawn's sharp light,
Both longing for the quiet cool of night?

After the first hours of celebration
(Embarrassed queries, brief exchange of news,
And courteous considered recognition
Of lasting ties we would not wish to lose)
We lapse into long spells of silence.
My brother acts correctly, and yet shows
A bashful eagerness, a tender patience
Towards the child, whose gladness overflows.
How sudden, binding, strange and solemn
This new responsibility must be;
How blank the sense of intervening time
To one who never saw her infancy!
Benumbed by what has happened, what has changed,
He hides beyond my reach, cold and estranged.

Nine years ago, when war was first declared,
Domestic plans were shattered and I left
To find us money. I was un-prepared
For separation. Guilty, stunned, bereft,
Eventual return was for a while
My only aim; but with the years my love
Has faded. Now, to watch her anxious smile
Is to be trapped with no chance of reprieve.
How strange it is to fear myself traduced
By the spent passion of those long-gone nights
On finding my own features reproduced
In Caroline our daughter – who by rights
Has first claim on my duty and affections.
Oh to undo, not resurrect, my actions!

ANNETTE'S IMPRESSIONS OF WILLIAM

He seems a lot less ravaged by the years
Than I. But has *he* raised a child, or borne
Opprobrium, or suffered daily fears
For safety, trapped inside his native town?
After a week together we both know
How little of each other's lives we share.
Nine years are not expunged – we surely grow
No younger as we lay our fond hearts bare,
And no whit closer. Proud Napoleon,
Whose deeds we curse and criticise so often,
Commands the only ground we have in common:
My royalist allegiance will not soften,
While principles that William once held dear
Look set to topple soon and disappear.

The day is hot, the courtyard stinks, there are
Two old witches spying from their window
As we come and go. We have English guests
Here with us for a while – Maman reminds me
I must call Monsieur Williams 'Papa'.
She taught him French till I was born,
But he speaks SO slowly and can barely
Understand a word I say! My auntie
Brought two gifts for me: a china doll
From London and this notebook, to write
What I think and see each day. Tonight
They stay up late to talk about the dangers
Maman has run – and 'Boney' who they hate.
We will not go tomorrow to the fête.

WILLIAM, ON NAPOLEON'S BIRTHDAY

In every city, town, and village square
As if to mock the hollow name which once
Rang bravely out synonymous with France
Crowds gather, thickening the foetid air
Like flies over a stinking pool of cess.
They meet in servile and unthinking glee
To fête Napoleon whose tyranny
They ratify. Ah, fond hopes, fade and cease!
The past is like a fortress deaf and blind
Whose every entrance under lock and key
Defies my penetration. Now consigned
To blank oblivion, the name of liberty
Is dead. Most citizens are meek, resigned
To watch the last leaves falling from the tree.

A GAP IN DOROTHY'S JOURNAL

The journal is inhibited, revealing
No hint, after a strange and sore decade,
Of how he made amends – no clue to feelings
Tumultuous or strained on either side.
What passed between the poet and Annette
(While Caroline sat still, or talked
In French with 'auntie' Dorothy) is private
Here, as it was there discreetly tucked
Away. For years they'd corresponded,
Worked patiently on each side to ensure
A fair arrangement, always closely bonded
By fondness and respect that would endure.
How soon, behind closed doors, was it agreed
What could be spared by him, and what she'd need?

If I could give a voice to loneliness
I would not do it now, while he is here.
I might succumb to grievance or distress
And little Caroline might overhear.
Besides, I am too proud. He is not mine.
I have known this for many a long year.
Our daughter is not newly born, but nine:
Our love affair is past – not worth a tear.
And yet, and yet, new sentiments are woken
By this strange visit with his chaperone.
No deed is done, no word is ever spoken
Without her knowledge. We should be alone.
What might still happen if for just one night
I met him privately, and out of sight?

'a hundred thousand sparkles balls shootings, & streams of glowworm light'

Nothing to do in this drab seaside town.
Trapped in a maze of dirty streets we saw
The shadows shrink then slowly lengthen
Like stray cats stretched asleep against shut doors.
At night we felt the magic of the harbour
Where far off in the bright and beckoning west
Like a white cloud crested high with Dover
Castle, we could glimpse the English coast.
We lingered here on calm hot nights to see
The little boats row out with wings of fire
And all the tracks of sail-boats streaming free.
Caroline walked with us by the shore
And chattered about glow-worm lights, excited –
I was so glad to find the child delighted.

This is the fourth week of my journal.
I am running out of things to say!
We found some crab-claws in the pool today
While Papa was pacing up and down
The beach, looking vaguely out to sea
And *muttering*. (He didn't notice me.)
My auntie and Papa sail home tomorrow.
I wonder will they come back here again?
They say the 'fragile peace' is soon to end:
The spies are all around us; only French ships
Leave the harbour, or come in. Maman
Agrees. She is exhausted, looking forward
To some quiet times at home with me.
I shall miss my walks with Auntie Dorothy.

A PURCHASE BEFORE LEAVING

The ring is Belgian: eighteen-carat gold.
I wonder, did he buy it while alone,
Or was his sister there to try the cold
Thing on, half-willing it to be her own?
Imagine as they stood there side by side
(A shuttered shop in Rue de la Tête d'Or)
And played the parts of nervous groom and bride,
Their only witness a French jeweller:
How tense she was, how tenderly
He held her wrist and drew the circle down
Her middle finger – then, how gingerly
She took it off, remembering that soon
(Though far away, and in another land)
It would fit snugly, on a different hand.

Did I think that by revisiting this place
I could put my past mistakes to rest
And be less haunted, leave behind no trace
Of having been here, an unwelcome guest?
What made me underestimate this test
Of courage, loyalty, and keen endurance?
Where'er I go, thin spectres of the past
Come back to mock me. Vanished is the France
In which I lived and loved; the place which once
Gave substance to a young impassioned dream.
I walk the streets of Calais in a trance,
Bewildered by an unremitting stream
Of memories and deafened by the tread
Of Consequence, a loud recurring dread.

ANNETTE, AFTER PARTING

More freely now than then my hot tears flow.
He stood beside the door just as he stood
That day in Orléans ten years ago,
But this time knowing that he left for good.
If I half hoped that he might change his mind,
It was naïve of me. He came resolved
To do what he must do; with this in mind
A painful visit has in part absolved
His guilt and put to rest the long dark years
Of separation and uncertainty.
How strange his absence as the slow day wears;
How distant he already seems to be,
As if a life slipped by between his going
And this new state of *clearly* knowing.

THE HOME CROSSING

'Dear fellow Traveller! Here we are once more…'

Did she protect the ring on their slow journey
And turn it tensely on her middle finger?
The sea is rough and she's sick all the way –
Upset, with wrenching stomach pains that linger
Long after she stands firm on English ground.
They bathe together, gaze back at Calais,
Rejoicing in familiar country sounds:
Bells ringing, a cock crowing, the homely
Music of a river flowing. He's glad, he says,
The Channel comes at last between them and
The 'frightful neighbourhood' of France. The days
Are gone for sympathy with that spent land.
She twists the ring and sends warm thoughts of peace
Across the Channel to her only niece.

WILLIAM, ON THE PROSPECT OF MARRIAGE

I learn too late that time is not my own.
Leased out, I am a house that overfills
With women. I will never be alone
Except by taking to the distant hills.
My sister, here beside me, now reclaims
The better part of me – which was on loan
Throughout this month. Three women's names
Have haunted me in France; two writ in stone.
I must move forward to embrace the life
That I have chosen willingly. But oh,
How guiltily I use that grave word, 'wife'
Which taunts – and, yes – even torments me so.
Annette, forgive me please and find repose.
Our chapter reaches now its awkward close.

PART SIX

In city pent

My brother, on the London coach, is writing
About a Negro woman met on board
While I (still feeling sick) am sitting
Beside him taking down his every word.
My mind is somewhere else throughout the day;
I store my worries in a private hoard.
Two weeks at most we planned to be away
So how is Mary doing all this time
And is she vexed by our unplanned delay?
Do letters reach her? Does the big hand climb
Reluctant, slow, tormenting, round the dial
As she expects the coming hour to chime?
Three further weeks to go – how will she while
The lonely time away through this long trial?

WILLIAM, ON NIGHT WALKS IN LONDON

'Sweet Thames run softly, till I end my song…'

At night I walk the dim-lit empty streets
Absorbing only intermittent sounds:
Cats scrimmaging, a watchman on his beat,
Faint footfalls magnified beyond the bounds
Of time and place. At first light I return
To spots along the river. Here I found
(In years gone by) replenishment. I yearn
For utter solitude yet every day
As London's clamour hems me in I turn
For company to Lamb, my prop and stay.
Without this gentle-hearted city guide
Nel mezzo del cammin I would lose my way
In unknown territory – trackless, wide,
Beset with dangers still on every side.

The days move quickly in a cheerful round
Of walks with Charles and Mary Lamb, who share
Their cherished London with us: they have found
Domestic bliss here, as we do in Grasmere.
Their rooms are spacious, comfortable, clean –
Away from noise and filth, the foggy air
That presses in all round us in the mean
Streets – overcrowded, narrow, grim – in which we
Spend some afternoons. The poverty seen
There, an open spectacle, is not to be
Ignored: my brother rails at splendour,
Luxury, excess and greed. Nights leave him free
To pace alone in darkness or to wander,
Companioned by the river's sweet meander.

CHARLES LAMB, ON WALKING WITH THE WORDSWORTHS

'In fine, I have satisfied myself that there is such a thing as that which tourists call romantic, which I very much suspected before, they make such a spluttering about it.'

Oh! Fleet Street and the Strand, how small I feel
In your *degrading* presence! The Wordsworths,
Just returned from Calais, walk with me,
Delighted by my former greatness.
Three weeks with Coleridge in Keswick were
Enough to prove to me that I was great,
Enveloped by a net of mountains, huge
Floundering bears and couchant sleeping
Monsters... Glorious creatures, fine old fellows,
Skiddaw and all, I shall not forget you!
But now, shrunk to my usual size, I guide
These wanderers about the *little* streets.
How furtively they walk, tight-lipped, as though
To guard some secret they must not let go.

We stand here on Westminster Bridge again,
Remarking on the beauty of the scene
And working at a sonnet he began
Before Calais. It seems that we have been
Too long away. Now here at last comes Lamb:
Breathless and hurrying, as always keen
To have us know that this great river's charm
And splendour must outlive – no, *supercede*
That of our Northern Lakes. 'For all their calm
They ain't a patch on *this*!' He gestures, freed
Into grandiloquence by our attention.
The time at long last comes for us to read
The sonnet out, and after some correction
Complete it – to Lamb's glowing satisfaction.

The Smithfield rabble shrieks as with one voice.
Trapped in a heaving shoving mass we cling
Together, swiftly carried without choice
Among the monkeys' loud brash chattering
To showmen's booths where fun is bought and sold.
At the inmost mongering bartering
Core of this hellish self-consuming world
We are prodded, pick-pocketed and cursed;
Then suddenly, as if in roughness hurled
From a small vessel, torn and tempest-tossed,
My sister is detached and borne away
Further and yet further until all but lost
In a huge swirling roaring human sea,
Her calm eyes fixed like steadfast lights on me.

Far off across a crowded market square
I catch Lamb's humorously candid eye.
He grins then waves, as if to send good cheer.
Now I am jostled, elbowed, swept away
By forces stronger than my feeble will
Like bobbing driftwood carried by the sway
Of mighty currents...Waiting for a lull
I struggle free down cobbled streets to where
A crowd has gathered round a sweetmeat stall
And landed in a doorway I rest there.
The fairground mood is catching and it starts
Me tapping with my foot. What can I hear?
A ballad singer propped against his cart
Gives me 'John Barleycorn' with all his art.

What a deal of fuss he makes when parted
From his sister for a single worried hour!
I tremble for his spirits when once started
On matrimony's long demanding *tour*.
And how he rails at London's bustling noise –
Lord! Has he never seen a crowd before?
How tense and jittery he seems these days.
Has Calais robbed him of his former calm
Or has he been too long and far away,
Deprived of hearth and home, the daily balm
Of nearby lakes and old familiar hills
Which never interfere or do him harm?
Will marriage be the cure for all his ills –
Remorse, anxiety, the 'fear that kills'?

DOROTHY, ON BEING REUNITED WITH HER
BROTHER JOHN

How glad we feel, all three, to be at last
Together. We have spent too long apart!
And yet our dearest John is overcast,
As if some trouble played about his heart.
Perhaps financial worries weigh him down,
A venture he is timorous to start?
He talks with eager fondness of our own
Dear garden, which he helped to dig and sow –
And of the path he must now make alone.
'The ferns beside the steps – do they still grow?
Do you still walk the grove named after me
Reciting verses, pacing to and fro?'
How keenly he brings back the memory
Of that first year! How close we were, all three.

LAMB, OBSERVING DOROTHY WITH HER
BROTHERS

Her 'wild' eye darts 'twixt one and t'other still,
Astir and warming under every glance
As if her heart could never get its fill!
The bonds of love, disturbed in childhood once,
Have been re-forged and now are just as strong
As if these three, conjoined in pleasant dance,
Had tripped in unison their whole life long –
And why would any woman not be glad
To time her steps to those of Sailor John,
Who is not haughty, dull, morose or sad?
I see now how this little Grasmere clan
Survives, and thrives. It would be more than bad
If such a nest were broken in upon
By neighbours, interlopers – anyone!

JOHN, ON HIS BROTHER'S IMMINENT MARRIAGE

Meeting in London, where I always feel
Unsettled, mention of his wedding plans
Has shaken me. I wish dear Mary well,
But I am haunted still – do all I can –
By tender hours that she and I have known.
Not long ago, a silent cautious man,
I relished every walk we took alone.
Was it so wrong to hope that one day *we*
Might wed? Perhaps. And now those days are gone
My mind is overcome with vain regret,
With fretful wayward thoughts that fondly yearn.
Her wedding-day has long ago been set.
Now passed beyond the point of no return,
Too late for happiness, I live and learn.

Many a time he talked of his 'dear
Mary' then, his feelings shyly slipping out.
They walked alone so much in that first year
With us at Grasmere – I have little doubt
That they were close, though not quite courting.
He must regret that they have grown apart,
The life with me that she will soon be starting.
He mentions that he feels his spirits low,
And names his worst of fears – departing
Never to see us more. We cannot know
What his forthcoming trip will bring: he leads
A dangerous life at sea and now must go.
What deep distress this parting with him breeds
In we who fail to meet his hopes and needs.

JOHN'S LETTER

Dearest Mary, my stay in London will
End tomorrow. I will soon be sailing.
My brother and my sister are both well.
They send their dearest, fondest greetings.
(We dined at Montague's tonight. I shall
Settle financial matters in the morning
And hope that on returning I prove still
Prosperous…) I have, meanwhile, been reading
Your letter over and over – yes, till
Tears have come into my eyes, and I
Know not how to express my feelings!
Truly thou art a dear kind creature.
Whatever fate befall me I will always love
And bear thy memory with me to the grave.

WILLIAM IN DOROTHY'S SICK-ROOM, 18 SEPTEMBER

Whether from homesickness or agitation,
Long travel, London's fog and fretful stir,
My sister has succumbed now to exhaustion.
She worsens, thins and pales; the doctors fear
Pneumonia. Confined to bed, she spends
Her days beside the open window where
This evening's blood-red harvest moon now lends
Its glory to her rationed patch of sky.
We talk of home in summer and she sends
Her love to Coleridge, but wonders why
The dear man is not here himself, to show
Us how to eulogise the moon? We try,
But nothing comes. How agonising, slow
And drear these sickroom hours when no words flow.

PART SEVEN

The ring

GALLOW HILL, 24 SEPTEMBER

Tom's standing on the corn-cart forking corn
And Mary's waiting there – the bride-to-be.
She's watched out nervously all afternoon
But she looks fat and well, says Dorothy.
The pilgrims settle in at Gallow Hill
Where all are busy still with food and harvest.
Relieved to have arrived they wait a while
Before they eat, for they're in need of rest
And peace and privacy. But where's the ring?
She checks it's safe, still hidden in her luggage,
Then takes to bed, unwell and day-dreaming
Of Grasmere, what's to come, and Coleridge...
Tired out, in bed for days, she's not aware
That time is passing – that they all prepare.

DAWN AT THE FARM, SEPTEMBER

'Happy as I am, I half dread that concentration of all tender feelings, past, present and future which will come upon me on the wedding morning.'

Oh! The joy of waking here once a long
Drench of sleep has washed away all care.
A cock crows at first light; then birdsong
Saturates the warm September air.
What sweet relief to hear the normal stir
Of farm life as routines begin again,
A sound so tranquil that it might repair
The blank uncounted miseries of men.
I soon must face the wedding day and then
We two will go to Town End at long last
And bring dear Mary with us, to remain.
Until the next few anxious days are past
The ring stays quietly in my possession.
I keep it safe, a lingering concession.

COLERIDGE, AFTER A NIGHTMARE

'I dreamt of Dorothy, William & Mary – and that Dorothy
was altered in every feature…'

They are away from here. The night before
The wedding day I dream of Dorothy
Who *looms,* obese and ugly with red hair.
Three times she mutters what I know already:
She is transformed. She is no more *herself*
In this disturbing dream than I am still
At school, as I would hate to be. In stealth
She morphs into a pale and frightful
Hag who *hounds* me, trying to pass on
Her foul disease by breathing in my face.
Appalled, I wake and write the nightmare down,
Deploring secretly what comes to pass
On this, the seventh anniversary
Of my disastrous fateful wedding-day.

'A grief without a pang, void, dark, and drear,
A stifled, drowsy, unimpassioned grief,
Which finds no natural outlet, no relief,
In word, or sigh, or tear...'

Does Coleridge intend to cast a pall
Over this quiet Yorkshire wedding,
Or is 'Dejection' published as a call
For help, a desperate way of spreading
His need for a more sympathetic ear?
How strange to think that in the *Morning Post*
His poem will be clearly blazoned there.
How shocking for us all, this new outburst,
Yet nothing can be done to set it right!
I know so well his feelings at this time
And cannot think he does it out of spite.
He may be hurt, aggrieved, but not malign.
To cast him as Iago makes no sense;
The timing is a sad coincidence.

A CEREMONY, 4 OCTOBER

'At a little after 8 o clock I saw them go down the avenue
towards the Church. William had parted from me up stairs. I
gave him the ring – with how deep a blessing! I took it from
my forefinger where I had worn it all the night before – he
slipped it again onto my finger and blessed me fervently.'

Who does the ring belong to on the day?
She's writing this at home a few weeks later:
This is her journal; here she has her say –
But is she a reliable narrator?
'Fervently' he blessed the thin gold ring
But watch him as he gives it back again!
Now, even now, the morning of the wedding,
He's at it still – the same old teasing game:
Still granting restitution, still pretending
That their lives will always stay the same.
How firmly she removes the blessèd thing,
How cruelly he gives it back again.
What brinkmanship the very day he's wed
And takes another woman to his bed!

'Flesh of my flesh' he'd said, 'bone of my bone.'
And so she'd worn it like a talisman,
Never to part, never to lose her home,
Not even when the next new phase began.
Now, even now, it passes to and fro
Between 'dear sister' and much dearer brother.
See how she wills herself to let it go,
See how it reclaims her – as his lover?
'With all my worldly goods I thee endow'.
So the ring pledges as it's lightly passed
From hand to hand – both then and now,
As if still undecided to the last.
You'd almost think it had life of its own.
Flesh of her flesh indeed – bone of her bone.

AFTER THE WEDDING BREAKFAST

The bells have rung, the bride and groom are here;
The mood is festive and the day is fine.
Brisk in the kitchen, spreading her good cheer,
Sara prepares a meal and pours the wine.
There are no gifts, no ceremonial
Toasts; but William shows his sympathy
For Mary as she bids the farm farewell
Supported by her sister, Dorothy.
When seated in the coach, all three together,
Their dawning sense of all she'll sorely miss
Can't spoil the joy that each feels in the other,
Watched by their family in happiness.
The ring is there on Mary's finger now –
All eyes rejoicing in its steady glow.

Four years ago, when journeying to Grasmere,
We tramped the frozen roads of Wensleydale
In snow's bright stillness, and not far from here
Climbed up beneath the mighty waterfall
To watch it crashing in its icy pool.
Transported now alongside stubble-meadows
Edged with thick hawthorns, elms, and dry-stone walls
Where becks are quiet, dawdling in shadows,
We are enveloped in the warming glow
Of autumn's bronzes, cradled dreamily
And rocked by steady motion till the slow
Hypnotic wash of dream and memory
Seduces us, all three, to sleep at last
Among the murmuring waters of the past.

DOROTHY DREAMS OF HARDRAW SCAR

From the high fells you carve your wayward course
And now in a single sudden chute you fall:
Noisy and fierce, a mighty thunderous force,
Releasing your pent power, your strength, your all
In this dark hollow where I stand confronted
By a huge cavernous and echoing wall
Scooped out around your form in sedimented
Layers of limestone, sandstone, shale.
No seedling could settle long enough here
To root itself, no climber find a stay
In the serrated sides which drop sheer
To the beck as it tumbles down the valley.
But I can walk beneath you, see you batter
The shining rocks below, or watch the way
You smash and in perpetual motion shatter
Your own reflection with dancing froth and spray.

WILLIAM, ON REVERIE

*'The water shot directly over our heads into a basin, and among
the fragments wrinkled over with masses of ice as white as
snow...'*

We have heard Hardraw roaring and have seen
From that cavernous and dripping space
The whole wide valley shimmer through a veil
Of falling water. But years have come between
Our recollections and the slippery place,
Dreams day by day supplanting what was real.
Have we lost our way then, trying to re-trace
Our journey through this dale to Grasmere?
The distance closes and I cannot tell
Who writes these words in hazy motion here,
      So bodiless I feel.

A HONEYMOON TABLEAU

'Wm fell asleep, lying upon my breast & I upon Mary. I lay
motionless for a long time, but I was at last obliged to move.'

M's squashed inside the snug close-fitting carriage,
The lowest person in this pile of three –
A strange position after recent marriage,
No sign of any struggle to break free.
D's too worn-out by travelling to grumble
But feels a crushing weight upon her chest;
She's thinking of the coming rough and tumble
Of wedded life (and if it's for the best).
William, well-cushioned on his travels,
Sleeps soundly and is none the worse for wear,
Contented that his plan has not unravelled,
Convinced that all arrangements have been fair.
Transport them, driver, safely home to bed –
The watchful sister and the newly wed.

I doze, like a napping cat. While half asleep
I see my brother Tom arriving home
From fields nearby. He drives a cart heaped
High with hay. I wake, and long to be alone.
She is present alongside us always,
Recalling earlier times and younger days
(Her longest and her happiest journeys)
With all the tenderness that love betrays.
Oh! Farewell, now, to vanished pleasures –
All she has thought and noticed, written, stored
Becomes a trove of common treasures
Which once was cherished as a private hoard.
Our lives are intertwined, and come what may
Today is sundered now from yesterday.

WILLIAM, ON FULFILMENT

Could I stop time anywhere it would be
Just before arriving, as we descend
The hill at dusk and all together see
The fertile waters of our dear homeland
Unfolding there before us without end.
Three months of arid absence lead at last
To this glad moment as the carriage wends
Its slow way downward. And what need of haste
As we anticipate a rapt foretaste
Of absolute possession? That rich dower
Of pleasure will too soon be in the past
And a remembered thing; but for one hour
No sweeter bliss in this dark world and wide
Than to be heading homeward, side by side.

PART EIGHT

Home at Grasmere

TOWN END, 6 OCTOBER

Every homecoming brings back the way
They first arrived, an oft-revolving wheel
That turns and settles where it's meant to stay.
But this time what the travellers think and feel
In candle-lit procession round the garden
Is hard to know; they're all so tired and quiet.
Each is subdued. Each has a hidden
World of hopes and fears as their first night
Draws in. Brother and sister both move
Slowly, as in dream, remembering
The brooms, the laurels, all the trees they love
As they were before the summer's growing.
What thick profusion of dark leaves they meet
Along the orchard path, their shared retreat!

How strange to think of them at home in bed
After so long away. Three months have passed.
I am left out of all they did and said –
A wilful child who is denied their trust.
While they were gone I scrambled up the hills
And watched the moon from river, lake and moor;
I followed becks up the remotest fells
And heard the ghylls among the mountains roar;
I found my way to hidden tarns and valleys –
Then most contented when I stood alone
Beneath the dark of loud tempestuous skies
And watched the rain beat hard on rock and stone.
My short-lived freedom gone, I am bereft:
Reduced to what I was before they left.

SARA COLERIDGE, ON HER HUSBAND'S STATE
OF MIND

For three months we preserved our fragile peace:
He has been settled; I submissive, meek.
But now his so-called friends are back again
The Black Drop opens a profound abyss
And down he goes – immersed within a week,
His brave reforms and promises in vain!
Our days will now be restless, all our nights
Destroyed by loud recurring shrieks
As he submits to dark despair and pain.
Oh, God! Please grant me strength to face this fight
                And keep us sane.

It was a perfect day, almost till the end.
We went to Easedale as a family
(William, myself and Mary) to see
As many waterfalls as we could find,
And cool streams tumbling down hidden glens –
Delighted to be back, glad to be free,
The clear blue sky a perfect ministry,
Sun warm and high among the mountains.
They went ahead of me to find the tarn
And I was left in solitary silence.
We hoped to find him here on our return,
Enthused to see us all, a ready audience,
But he seems sad: withdrawn and secretive,
With little to communicate or give.

WILLIAM, ON A PUBLICATION BY COLERIDGE

'My father confessor is meek and holy,
Mi Fili, still he cries, peccare noli,
And yet how oft I find the pious man
At Annette's door, the lovely courtesan!'

Whatever has possessed our dearest friend
To make this shocking, low and mischievous
Suggestion? Will he never bring an end
To such defamatory talk? Grievous
His need to hurt, to mar our glad return
With this vile exhibition of his spite!
I pace the orchard path in anger, yearn
To calm him, and to put our conflicts right.
With time, with patience, reason will prevail...
I see that he was writing many a verse
While we were all away. Not much can ail
Him then; God knows that we have seen him worse.
Oh! Spot so tranquil, may your healing balm
Soon mend his spirits, keep us safe from harm.

No room inside his heart of any kind
For me who loved him and who gave him ease
With tales and ballads long as you might please,
Inventions no one else could make or find.
He left me long ago and far behind:
So starved of happiness my touch might freeze
The women who now swarm like honey-bees
Around the hive of his prolific mind.
How large is their capacity for love?
Triple the blow, yes triple the living hell
If Asra comes to live with him as well;
Then is no respite from the gods above.
See, his return unmans and fells me quite.
My heart is broken. Nothing puts it right.

He takes the marriage ill, and feels shut out
From all that the new couple do and say.
I fear he has succumbed to a fresh bout
Of misery each time he stays away.
I feel for him, so bitter and cast down,
As if I know his thoughts from the inside –
And watch for every furrow, every frown,
Each sign of envy or of wounded pride.
This used to be a home for him as well,
A place where he could come and speak his woes
But now there is no tale that he will tell
That does not make the three of us his foes.
Dear Coleridge, I'd teach you if I could
How you might love us, if you only would.

'On Friday 8th we baked Bread, & Mary & I walked, first
upon the Hill side, & then in John's Grove, then in view of
Rydale, the first walk I had taken with my Sister.'

Kind Dorothy assists me settling in,
Arranging walks to soothe me, making sure
That after travelling I will begin
To value old routines and sights once more.
With quick facility she helps me trace
Thoughts that lead homeward in a steady line;
And how could I *not* love this homely place
Where her domestic life is also mine?
Today, in John's Grove, she and I were talking
Of friends and days gone by. How many
Sweet contented hours I can recall, walking
With Sara, William, John and Dorothy
All round the glittering lake of Grasmere;
But now I miss dear Tom and wish him here.

WILLIAM, IN JOHN'S GROVE

And so in marriage our blest lives converge,
Our long uncertainties at last resolved.
But as I walk this woodland ground again
To find the place where two tracks used to merge,
The memory that one who was involved
Is now excluded brings a sense of pain:
My brother often paced this lonesome grove
And made a narrow path, long since dissolved –
Which, thinking of him on the wat'ry main,
I loved to visit. *Two* were wont to rove
      Here – their attachments plain…

Does he ever wonder, as I sometimes do,
What it would involve to *be* another?
In John's Grove daily, pacing to and fro,
He surely misses his sea-faring brother;
But has it struck him that this story might
Be ending otherwise, and *just as well?*
If John had stayed with them for one more night
And made a match with Mary…who can tell?
If all that I suspect can be believed
Then there are several different ways
In which contentment might have been achieved
Within these interwoven families.
My sympathy is with you, sailor John –
Shut out, unrecompensed, still wandering on.

DOROTHY, ON RESUMING HER JOURNAL

I steal an hour or two from household chores
To hide upstairs inside my quiet room
And write my Grasmere journal, which last paused
Three months ago. (The strongest sense of home
Floods in when I am most alone.) Our cottage fills
With smell of bread-loaves freshly baked, still warm.
Outside, my brother clears the leaf-strewn well
With Mary's help. The afternoon is calm,
Their laughter drifting through the open door
With memories of spring. I hesitate
In writing, mention only what I saw,
Not what was said; my sentiments are private.
How warily, unsure what I will find,
I feel my way in words to reach the end.

FUGUE

'I kept myself as quiet as I could, but when I saw the two men running up the walk, coming to tell me it was over, I could stand it no longer....'

No, she cannot watch. Her courage falters.
Over again, long after they are wed,
Her mind turns round, as with the might of waters.
She sees herself there – prostrate on the bed;
This is the dreaded hour, the blank hiatus –
The ring unseen, the vows unheard, unsaid,
No memory but strangeness. Nothing alters:
No sights or sounds, she might as well be dead.
And now, returning warmth and light and feeling.
They're home, they're married, it's all over.
But still her life's in shock, her senses reeling.
Once reunited, was she carried by her brother
Across that other threshold? No one knows:
Onward like a stream the journal flows.

COLERIDGE, SEEKING SOLACE

Look not for feeling, sympathy and heart
Where most you might expect it. There it palls,
Resistant to each blandishment, each art
Which rises like a prayer and then falls.
We who in matrimony find no joy
Must seek our solace in transcendent things.
The mind that knows no bounds can never cloy;
Its disembodied spirit soars and sings.
To everything on earth there is a season.
Come rain come shine the stars are still above,
Beyond our ken, beyond our human reason –
And so, dear Asra, is eternal love.
Without its guidance I am lost at sea:
A drifting barque, unless you pity me.

WILLIAM, THINKING AHEAD

The golden leaves are turning now to brown
And, shaken from the trees, red windfalls lie
Along the orchard pathway, bruised and strewn.
Across the lake the last few swallows fly
And cheerful robins hop from stone to stone
Pecking at crumbs we dropped, then flit on high.
Among all restless things we three alone
Are settled, glad to have each other nigh.
Our month in Calais now long gone, we hear
Good news from there, and much there is to bring
Fresh hope in this and every future year.
Quite soon, if all goes well, new life will spring
Not only all around, from hill and dale,
But here at Town End, centre of the vale.

DOROTHY, AFTER A WALK TO RYDAL, 31 OCTOBER

John Monkhouse called. Wm & S went to Keswick...'

I walked alongside Mary up the hill
To look at Rydale. I was much affected,
Alighting on a bar of Sara's gate,
By beauty. All was perfect, tranquil, still.
The sun shone evenly on hill and dale;
The distant birch trees were like golden flowers,
The fields a sober brown. All colours
Melted warmly inside our fertile vale.
No tone was bright, distinct or separate.
When lunch was done we both lay on the floor,
Side by dear side, in the cool parlour's quiet.
She slept, but my mind shifted like a door
That is ajar. At dusk we sat together –
As if we had been here in peace for ever.

THE MANUSCRIPT

'William had parted from me up stairs. I gave him the ring –
with how deep a blessing! I took it from my forefinger where
I had worn it all the night before – he slipped it again onto
my finger and blessed me fervently...I kept myself as quiet as
I could, but when I saw the two men running up the walk,
coming to tell me it was over, I could stand it no longer, &
threw myself on the bed where I lay in stillness, neither hearing
nor seeing any thing, till Sara came upstairs to me & said, 'they
are coming.''

As if to break a silence that they chose
The firmly blacked-out lines give her away.
The full force of her feeling wrought those
Words, expressing all she needed then to say.
Who was it tried to hide her rite of passage,
Protecting someone from its truth and pain?
Only infra-red could pierce the message,
Revealing this strange ritual again.
The ink is iron-based. No later hand
Has tampered with her thoughts. Then was it she,
As she looked back, who shrank from their sharp sting, and
Scored them through in black so thoroughly –
That no one after all these years might tell
What she had felt that day and knew full well?

Notes to the poems

Dorothy observes, 15 April 1802
Eusemere (home of the Wordsworths' friends Thomas and Catherine Clarkson) is at the head of Ullswater.

Dorothy, on arriving
The epigraph is from W.W.'s long poem in blank verse, 'Home at Grasmere', mostly composed in 1800.

Dorothy, on local attachments
D.W. lists the closest members of the Wordsworth Circle – her brother John, Mary Hutchinson (W.W.'s wife-to-be) and S.T.C. These three people feature in connection with particular local spots in W.W.'s 'Poems on the Naming of Places' (published in *Lyrical Ballads* 1800.)

William, on sharing memories
The epigraph is from W.W.'s poem 'The Sparrow's Nest', composed in 1802.

Dorothy, on dead times
'A little prattler among men' – D.W. quotes from 'The Sparrow's Nest', in which W.W. remembers his sister in her infancy at Cockermouth, surrounded by her four brothers. D.W. was separated from her family at the age of six, following her mother's death, and did not see her brothers again for nearly nine years. She grew up with an aunt and cousins in Halifax.

William's promise

The epigraph is from W.W.'s long blank-verse poem 'Home at Grasmere'.

Children in the wood

The epigraph is a quotation from the Grasmere Journal, 29 April 1802.

This sonnet alludes to a well-known ballad about two children, a brother and sister, who were abandoned by servants of their wicked uncle and died together in a wood, later to be buried under leaves by a robin.

William's dream

The epigraph is a quotation from the Grasmere Journal, 1 May. I have invented the dream.

William, Ars Poetica

The epigraph is from *The Prelude* (1805) Book XIII.

William, seeking a perfect form

In a letter to Alexander Dyce in 1833, Wordsworth wrote: 'In the better half of [Milton's] sonnets, the sense does not close with the rhyme in the eighth line, but overflows into the second portion of the metre. Now it has struck me, that this is not done merely to gratify the ear by variety and freedom of sound, but to aid in giving that pervading sense of intense Unity in which the excellence of the Sonnet has always seemed to me mainly to consist.' He went on to explain that he believed a sonnet 'ought to have a beginning, a middle and an end, like the three parts of a syllogism', and that he found it cumbersome to think of the 'architecture' of sonnets: 'I have been much in the habit of preferring the image of an orbicular body, – a sphere, or a dew-drop.'

Walking with Coleridge
Greta Hall – Coleridge's house in Keswick.

Coleridge, walking alone
The epigraph is a quotation from Coleridge's Notebooks. This sonnet is a 'cut-up' or 'cento', composed of sentences taken from 6 separate Notebook entries made by S.T.C. in 1802.

William, on 'The Rock of Names'
Members of the Wordsworth circle could not have anticipated what would later happen to the rock by Wythburn into which they had cut their initials. A plaque by Thirlmere (the reservoir which replaced Wythburn) reads as follows: 'THE ROCK OF NAMES / Fragments of a rock on which William Wordsworth Samuel Taylor Coleridge and their friends had carved their initials 1801–1802 were preserved by Canon Rawnsley in a cairn at this spot 1886-1984. / They were given by the North West Water Authority to the Dove Cottage Trust in 1984 and may be seen incorporated in a rock face behind the Grasmere and Wordsworth Museum. / The original 'Rock of Names' lay beside the lake and was blown up in constructing the much larger modern reservoir.'

Under Helvellyn, 4 May
The epigraph is a quotation from the Grasmere Journal, 4 May.

Coleridge, on living with his wife
This is a 'cut-up' sonnet, composed by using short excerpts from S.T.C.'s letters and notebooks.

Coleridge, yearning for Sara Hutchinson
Another 'cut-up', using excerpts from S.T.C.'s notebooks.

Sara Hutchinson was the sister of William's wife-to-be. Asra was S.T.C.'s private name for her.

Coleridge, on marriage
The epigraph is a quotation from a Notebook entry by S.T.C.

Ironically, Sara Hutchinson had the same name as S.T.C.'s wife. Sarah Coleridge (née Fricker) had changed her name to Sara at his request.

William, reassuring Coleridge
The epigraph is a quotation from *The Prelude*, Book XIII.

'Nether Stowey and Alfoxden' – S.T.C. and the Wordsworths had lived as neighbours in the Quantocks (he at Nether Stowey and they nearby at Alfoxden House) in 1797-8. It was during this year of close friendship that their collaborative volume *Lyrical Ballads* was put together.

Coleridge, on memories of 1798
The epigraph is from S.T.C.'s poem 'The Nightingale', written in 1798 at Nether Stowey and published in *Lyrical Ballads* 1798.

William attempts to console
The quotation is from W.W.'s poem 'The Leechgatherer', which in its revised and published form is known as 'Resolution and Independence'.

Dorothy, on medicine
'Spirit of water…sunshiny shower…' these phrases are from an entry in the Grasmere Journal, 24 November 1801.

Coleridge lets off steam
The epigraph is a quotation from a S.T.C. Notebook entry.

William, on friendship with Coleridge
The epigraph is a quotation from the Preface to Wordsworth's sonnet sequence about the River Duddon.

Coleridge, on Wordsworth's women
'Bit of fluff' – a disparaging reference to Annette Vallon. S.T.C. was later to refer to her as 'the lovely courtesan' in a poem which caused W.W. considerable hurt.

A conversation with Coleridge
The epigraph is a quotation from S.T.C.'s 'Letter to Sara Hutchinson' (the first version of his poem 'Dejection: an Ode'). Derwent Coleridge was his second surviving son, Berkeley having died as an infant while he was in Germany in 1799.

Coleridge, on thinking
This un-rhyming sonnet is a 'cut-up' composed from several separate letters written by S.T.C. in 1801–02.

Dorothy, sky-gazing 6 May
The epigraph is from S.T.C.'s 'Letter to Sara Hutchinson'. In the opening of that poem, S.T.C. refers to the 'Ballad of Sir Patrick Spens', where the lines 'I saw the old moon / With the new moon in her arms' are taken as a prefiguration of coming disaster.

'Our brother John' – John Wordsworth, youngest sibling in the family, was a sailor. He would later lose his life in a shipwreck off the coast of Dorset.

Coleridge, on love and friendship
This sonnet is a 'cut-up', composed of four different descriptions in S.T.C.'s Notebooks, which I have threaded together and given an allegorical twist.

William appeals to his friend
'One Life' – a phrase used frequently by W.W. and S.T.C. in their writings, especially during the 1790s, to allude to the doctrine that a divine spirit animates all things in the natural world. S.T.C. was more strongly inclined to believe in this idea than WW, having come under the influence of the Unitarian Joseph Priestley.

Coleridge retaliates
'you forget that it takes three…' S.T.C.'s supernatural ballad 'Christabel', intended for inclusion in *Lyrical Ballads* 1800, had remained incomplete. (This collection was published under W.W.'s name, whereas *Lyrical Ballads* 1798 had been a collaborative and anonymous publication.)

The Recluse – a long philosophical poem begun by W.W. and never completed, despite (or perhaps because of) the pressure of S.T.C.'s continuous encouragement and enthusiasm.

William defends past actions
'Minor exclusion' – of 'Christabel' from *Lyrical Ballads* 1800.

Dorothy, on Milton's influence
'Numberless glow-worms…faery light' – in 'Scorn not the sonnet' W.W. uses the glow-worm as a metaphor for Spenser's reliance on this form: 'a glow-worm lamp,/ It cheered mild Spenser, called from Faery-land/ To struggle through dark ways'.

William, on reading aloud
The epigraph is a quotation from a blank verse fragment composed in Germany, 1798–99.

Owl and moon in Bainriggs, 13 June
The epigraph is a quotation from the Grasmere Journal, 13 June.

'It was thin, like a gold ring snapped in two' – a further reference to D.W.'s description of the moon on 8 March 1802.

William, on revising 'The Leech-gatherer', 14 June
The epigraph is from a letter written by the Wordsworths to Sara Hutchinson, who had complained that 'The Leech-gatherer' was tedious.

Gallow Hill – a farm, home of the Hutchinson family near Scarborough in Yorkshire.

Dorothy, on William's change of mind
The epigraph is another quotation from a letter written by the Wordsworths to Sara Hutchinson. D.W. is echoing W.W.'s sentiments in upholding the superiority of the first version of this poem, which was much closer to her description of the leech-gatherer in the Grasmere Journal. When finally published as 'Resolution and Independence', the poem had taken into account Sara Hutchinson's (and implicitly S.T.C.'s) critique.

William digests some good news, 20 June
The epigraph is a quotation from an entry in the Grasmere Journal for 18 June.

'Lowther is to clear his cousin's debts': The Wordsworths had been waiting since the death of their father for repayment of a substantial sum of money owed to them by his employer and landlord James Lowther, Earl of Lonsdale. This was paid off in 1802 by James's cousin Sir William Lowther, giving them for the first time a degree of financial security.

Mary Hutchinson, at Gallow Hill
Letters in the Wordsworth household were never private; the practice was to read them aloud. D.W. took charge of most letter-writing, with W.W. making occasional contributions.

Dorothy's farewell, 7 July
The epigraph is a quotation from W.W.'s poem 'A Farewell', composed in June-July 1802 as the Wordsworths' departure for France approached. This poem, which gave W.W. a lot of trouble, was referred to in the Grasmere Journal as 'the poem on going for Mary'.

A question, 14 July
The epigraph is a quotation from D.W.'s entry in the Grasmere Journal on 14 July.
  This sonnet is not based on a S.T.C. Notebook entry, but the quotation in the last line comes from a poem written by S.T.C. in 1798 ('Hexameters') in which he describes the Wordsworths as 'all in each other'.

Mary, on impending separation
Tom – Mary's brother, a farmer, to whom she was very close.

Dorothy, after a short stay in London
The epigraph is a quotation from the Grasmere Journal. W.W. and D.W. took the Dover coach on 31 July or 1 August, and D.W.'s later journal entry describing the early morning scene may have provided the basis for W.W.'s 1802 sonnet, 'Composed on Westminster Bridge'.

Calais in August
The epigraph is a quotation from the Grasmere Journal: see the end of the Calais section.

Annette's impressions of William

'Daily fears/For safety...' Annette Vallon was a counter-revolutionary, tried and nearly imprisoned on one occasion for her activities in Blois.

Caroline's first journal

I have invented the detail of D.W. giving a journal to Caroline.

Monsieur Williams – Annette Vallon referred to W.W. in letters as 'Williams'.

Dorothy, a retrospective view

The epigraph is a quotation from D.W.'s retrospective account of the trip to France, written up in the Grasmere Journal after they had returned to Town End in October.

The home crossing

The epigraph is a quotation from W.W.'s 'Composed in a Valley near Dover', written the day they landed in England.

The 'frightful neighbourhood' of France – an allusion to W.W.'s poem 'Near Dover, September 1802', which begins, 'Inland, within a hollow vale, I stood;/And saw, while sea was calm and air was clear,/The coast of France – the coast of France how near,/Drawn almost into frightful neighbourhood.'

William, on night walks in London

The epigraph is a quotation from Spenser's 'Prothalamion'.

nel mezzo del cammin – the first line of Dante's *The Inferno*, which has been translated, 'When I had journeyed half of our life's way'.

Charles Lamb, on walking with the Wordsworths

This sonnet draws on a letter from Lamb to Thomas Manning, 24 September 1802.

A friendly exchange, 3 September
W.W.'s sonnet 'Composed upon Westminster Bridge' was
in all likelihood begun before the trip to Calais, though he
identifies it as compose on this day. I have invented the con-
versation with Charles Lamb.

William, at Bartholomew Fair
The episode recounted here is my invention, but this sonnet
is based on the impressions of Bartholomew Fair that W.W.
conveys in the last part of Book VII of *The Prelude*.

Lamb, observing Dorothy with her brothers
'wild' – W.W. famously refers to D.W.'s 'wild' eyes in 'Lines
written a few miles above Tintern Abbey'.

John's letter
This sonnet uses some of the phrasing found in a letter
written by John Wordsworth to Mary Hutchinson on 12
September 1802.

Dawn at the farm, 28 September
The epigraph is a quotation from a letter written by D.W.
on 28 September.

Coleridge, after a nightmare
The epigraph is a quotation from S.T.C.'s Notebook entry,
written on 4 October, also the anniversary of his own
wedding to Sarah Fricker.

Coleridge's dejection
The epigraph is a quotation from 'Dejection: an Ode', which
was published in the *Morning Post* on 4 October 1802,
addressed to 'Edmund', a pseudonym for W.W. (to whom
an intermediate version of this poem had been addressed).

A crowded carriage
The epigraph is from D.W.'s retrospective account of the Wordsworths' honeymoon journey home in October.

Dorothy dreams of Hardraw Scar
The Wordsworths had visited Hardraw Scar, England's highest waterfall, on their way to set up home in Grasmere in 1799.

William, on reverie
The epigraph is a quotation from a letter that W.W. and D.W. wrote jointly to Coleridge on arriving in Grasmere, December 1799.

Sara Coleridge, on her husband's state of mind
The 'Black Drop' to which Sara here refers was a very strong concoction of laudanum to which S.T.C. had ready access.

Mary, on her first days at Grasmere
The epigraph is a quotation from the Grasmere Journal, Friday 8 October.

Dorothy, on being reunited with Coleridge
This sonnet is based on events that D.W. recorded in the Grasmere Journal on Monday 11 October.

William, on a publication by Coleridge
The epigraph is a quotation from 'Spots in the Sun', a mischievous poem published by S.T.C. in the *Morning Post* a week after W.W.'s wedding, in which the occurrence of the name 'Annette' was presumably no coincidence. D.W. mentions in the Grasmere Journal that William was 'much oppressed' on 19 October. Allowing time for the *Morning Post* to reach Ambleside, his mood may be explained by his having read 'Spots in the Sun'.

Dorothy, on resuming her journal
D.W. wrote the entire section of the Grasmere Journal that deals with the Calais trip and the wedding retrospectively, and it is not clear on which day in October she did this.

A walk to Rydal, 31 October
The epigraph is a quotation from the Grasmere Journal, 31 October.

The manuscript
The epigraph is a quotation from the Grasmere Journal.

D.W. (who is writing this journal entry many days after the events took place) describes the ritual performed by herself and W.W. on the morning of his wedding to Mary Hutchinson, 4 October 1802. Two sentences in the manuscript have been heavily deleted.

Acknowledgements

This book is dedicated to my dear friend Sandie Byrne, who has read every one of the 135 sonnets as I have drafted them, making numerous suggestions as well as offering constant encouragement. Wes Williams made time to give me detailed and very welcome advice about a draft of the whole sequence. Tony Brignull, Tom Clucas, Jared Campbell and Tom MacFaul have been very generous with their time and enthusiasm. To all these creative and scholarly friends, many thanks.

My thanks also to the Hall Writers' Forum, an online resource for members of St Edmund Hall. Many of its members have given feedback on various sonnets, and the supportive ethos of the forum is a constant delight. I could not have written the sequence without its community.

I am excited by the association of Carcanet and the Wordsworth Trust in this rather unusual project, and would like to thank Michael Schmidt, Michael McGregor and Jeff Cowton for their strong support. I am grateful to editor Andrew Latimer and the production team for their excellent attention to detail. Many thanks also to Richard Holmes for writing the Preface.

Lastly, thanks to my husband Martin and daughter Emma – who patiently and humorously tolerate my obsession with poetry.

Lucy Newlyn
Cornwall, August 2019